Published by Creative Education
P.O. Box 227, Mankato, Minnesota 56002
Creative Education is an imprint of
The Creative Company
www.thecreativecompany.us

Design and production by The Design Lab
Art direction by Rita Marshall
Printed by Corporate Graphics in the
United States of America

Photographs by Dreamstime (Eric Gevaert), Getty
Images (Ian Nichols, Kate Roberts), iStockphoto
(Guenter Guni, Phil Hess, Eric Isselée, Marcel Mooij,
Sharon Morris, William Murphy, Ricky Russ, Dave
Thomasnz)

Library of Congress Cataloging-in-Publication Data
Riggs, Kate.
Gorillas / by Kate Riggs.
p. cm. — (Amazing animals)
Summary: A basic exploration of the appearance,
behavior, and habitat of gorillas, Earth's largest apes.
Also included is a story from folklore explaining why
gorillas do little but eat and sleep.
Includes bibliographical references and index.
ISBN 978-1-60818-107-0
1. Gorilla—Juvenile literature. I. Title. II. Series.
QL737.P96R54 2012
599.884—dc22   2010049121

CPSIA: 081412 PO1602

9 8 7 6 5

GORILLAS

BY KATE RIGGS

CREATIVE EDUCATION

Like all apes, gorillas have flat noses

A gorilla is an ape. Apes are animals known as **primates**. There are four kinds of gorilla. They are named for where they live on the **continent** of Africa.

continent one of Earth's seven big pieces of land

primates humans and animals such as apes and monkeys that have big brains and hands that can grip things

Gorillas have big bodies and large heads. They have long, strong arms and hind legs that they use to walk. Gorillas have black or brownish hair covering their bodies.

*The knuckles of a gorilla's hands
touch the ground when they walk*

Male gorillas are larger than females. Males can stand 6 feet (1.8 m) tall and weigh up to 500 pounds (227 kg). Females are usually about 5 feet (1.5 m) tall and 200 pounds (90 kg).

Around age 12, the hair on a male's back turns white

Waterfalls are found in some forests where gorillas live

Most gorillas live in **mountain** forests. Some like to live far up a mountain. Others like to live lower down the mountain. Gorillas can be found in many countries in central and western Africa.

mountain a very big hill made of rock

Gorillas eat plants.

Bamboo, wild celery, and thistles are some of their favorite plants. They also like to eat some flowers, fruits, and bark from trees. Gorillas have sharp teeth that can tear through tough plants.

Wild celery is 1 of more than 100 plants gorillas eat

A mother gorilla has one baby at a time. Babies grow quickly. They drink their mothers' milk and eat leaves and fruits. Baby gorillas like to wrestle and play. Gorillas can live for about 35 years in the wild.

When gorillas play, they hold their mouths open

Members of a gorilla troop take care of each other

Gorillas live in family groups called troops. There can be 5 to 30 gorillas in a troop. An older male gorilla called a silverback leads the troop. He helps them find food. He protects the troop from **predators** such as leopards.

predators animals that kill and eat other animals

Gorillas spend most of their time eating and sleeping. Adult gorillas eat up to 60 pounds (27 kg) of food a day! Gorillas take a lot of naps during the day. At night, they sleep for 13 to 15 hours.

Most gorillas build a nest on the ground to sleep in

Some people go to Africa to see gorillas in the wild. National parks help protect the gorillas and other animals that live there. Most people see gorillas in zoos. It is fun to see these large apes up close!

Gorillas greet each other using actions and sounds

A Gorilla Story

Why do gorillas do nothing but eat and sleep all day long? People who lived near the Congo River in Africa had a story about this. Long ago, it rained so much that the river flooded. The gorillas helped all the animals get to dry ground—even the fish! But fish need water to live. All the other animals made fun of the gorillas for their mistake. From then on, gorillas stopped doing anything except eating and sleeping.

Read More

Nichols, Michael, with Elizabeth Carney. *Face to Face with Gorillas*. Washington, D.C.: National Geographic, 2009.

Simon, Seymour. *Gorillas*. New York: HarperCollins, 2008.

Web Sites

Enchanted Learning: Gorillas
http://www.enchantedlearning.com/subjects/apes/gorilla/Gorillacoloring.shtml
This site has gorilla facts and a picture to color.

Koko's Kids Club
http://www.koko.org/kidsclub/
Learn about a famous gorilla named Koko and her friends.

Index